PENGUIN LIFE

EVERYTHING, BEAUTIFUL

Ella Frances Sanders is a *New York Times* and internationally best-selling author and illustrator of four books, including *Eating the Sun* and *Lost in Translation*. She lives in a quiet slice of Scotland and spends a reasonable amount of time following patches of sunlight around the house.

Everything, Beautiful

A Guide to
Finding Hidden Beauty
in the World

ELLA FRANCES SANDERS

life

PENGUIN BOOKS

An imprint of Penguin Random House LLC
penguinrandomhouse.com

A Penguin Life Book

ISBN 9780143137061 (paperback)
ISBN 9780525508564 (ebook)

Printed in the United States of America
1st Printing

Set in Adobe Caslon Pro
Designed by Cassandra Garruzzo Mueller

For my best one

"... BEAUTY DOES NOT RESERVE

ITSELF FOR SPECIAL ELITE MOMENTS

OR INSTANCES;

IT DOES NOT WAIT FOR

PERFECTION

"BUT IS PRESENT ALREADY SECRETLY IN EVERYTHING . "

— JOHN O'DONOHUE

"THE TRULY PRECIOUS THINGS

ARE THOSE

WHICH FORM LADDERS REACHING

TOWARDS THE BEAUTY OF

THE WORLD,

OPENINGS ON TO IT . "

— SIMONE WEIL

"...ONE DEFINITION OF BEAUTY —

A SORT OF LIGHTHOUSE,

SOMEWHERE TO START."

— BAHAR ORANG

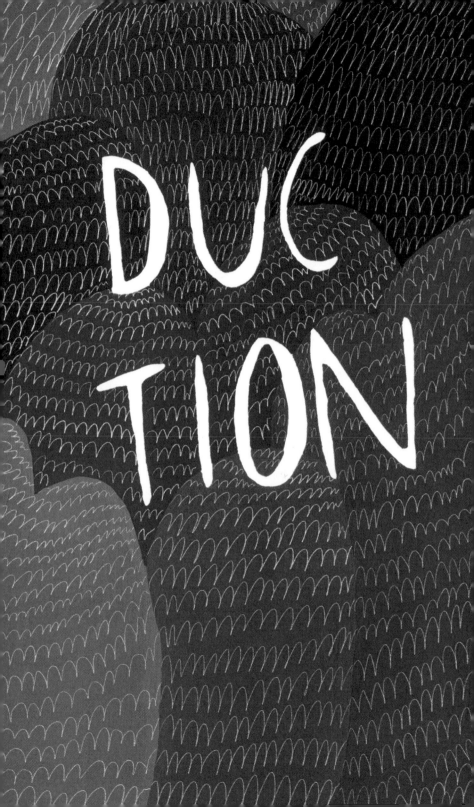

These days most of us are either constantly overwhelmed or getting very close to being constantly overwhelmed. And for those who do not feel overwhelmed in the slightest, there is usually a price being paid somewhere else. We are sent into spins of fear and feeling by all the things we need to get done, by the consequences of not doing those things, by the lack of time we have to process the deep and difficult happenings both in our close world and in the worlds of others, with the internet propelling us day in and day out toward noise, and comparison, and numbness. When the world feels unbearably large and largely out of control, what I've found is that there is almost always reassurance and meaning to be found in the smallest of things, in the smallest of beauties.

While paramedics scooped up my tiny grandmother after she had fallen in the garden, I noticed and tried to commit to memory the peach-like scent of the orange-honey-colored roses behind me. When feeling a hard-to-define homesickness after living in a country that felt like too-tight shoes, I was soothed by noticing migrating geese overhead, the dune grasses swaying in time to the sea, the color of mold on a lemon, the oddly synchronized pedaling of a large group of cyclists as they set off around a peninsula.

When you take the time
to see and hold these things,
you also begin to notice
how many other people do
not notice them. You
find yourself wanting to
take people by the arm and
point to skies, to horizons, to
new leaves on eucalyptus trees.
But I cannot blame people
for being unseeing when it
comes to beauty. As a thing
it has been overexposed and
covered in price tags and
sold through glossy, untrue
photos, and I do wonder
a lot if we have been
forced to look at one type
of beauty for so long that...

... we've completely forgotten how to see it in all its forms.

We currently live in a beauty drought. This isn't because the beauty isn't there, but rather because our current definitions of the word are not spacious or welcoming or inclusive, and because beauty has been pressed into strange, stale shapes by people and systems that do not have our best interests at their hearts—they don't have hearts, in a way. The word *beauty* has left most of us feeling confused, less than, and undeserving. Feeling that beauty has left us behind. Beauty has become something to buy, something to own, something to flaunt, but as I was reading just this morning while eating a piece of distinctly average cheesecake:

> "That's the thing about beauty, isn't it? In the end it belongs to everyone. In the end it belongs to no one except itself."*

---

* Susan Johnson

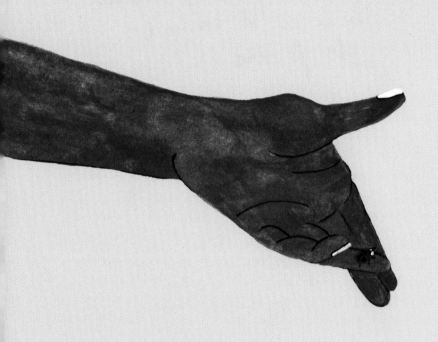

To me, beauty stands alongside love and gravity in holding the world together. From what I have observed, the only one of those we haven't picked apart is gravity, but with love and beauty we have taken shadowy, winding roads that have, in fact, led us away from love, away from beauty.

However impractical it may seem, I am going to try and help you find your way back to beauty. Simply because when we are held together by beauty, there is more room for liberation and less room for fear. More room for gentleness, appreciation, and empathy.

It won't be as simple or as instant as refreshing a website that is loading too slowly for your liking. Rather, it will be more like putting a delicate, very broken vase back together. But it is crucially important that we crawl back to beauty however we can, to find new definitions of beauty that allow us to be fully ourselves, powerfully noticing, and expansively human.

My hope is that this book is an antidote to fear, to darkness, to dullness, to overwhelm, to lost-ness, to sleeplessness, and to missing.

The definition of beauty, of beautiful, differs between countries, between cultures, and sometimes even between seconds. What society deems beautiful can change from one moment to the next, but for an individual, a particular beauty can sometimes stay forever.

SOMETIMES YOU WILL ENCOUNTER A PERSON, A PLACE, OR A THING,

AND YOU WILL CALL THAT PERSON, PLACE, OR THING BEAUTIFUL FOR THE

REST OF TIME.

PART
ONE

A BRIEF

HISTORY

OF

BEAUTY

HOW TO
EXPLAIN
BEAUTY

I would like to explain beauty as something a bit like music, a bit like water, a bit like love.

It was here before all of us and it will be here afterward, and during our brief, chaotic appointments with the planet, it does us extraordinary amounts of good to seek it out.

I could explain beauty as things that cause you to stop, but also as things that cause you to begin. I could go as far as to say that beauty is the invisible-visible force that makes things make sense, if only for a moment. I could explain it as the things that support the weight of our bodies. It might also be the reason why fish swim upstream, and the reason why we might choose to wake up next to the same person for sixty years.

I'd like to explain beauty as corridors before people fill them, as a sunrise seen only by birds. It is the thin lines we draw between ourselves and everything else : the making it make sense, the hindsight, the worthwhile, the looking forward, the acts of kindness, the hoping.
It is the rabbit making it across the car-streaked road in time.

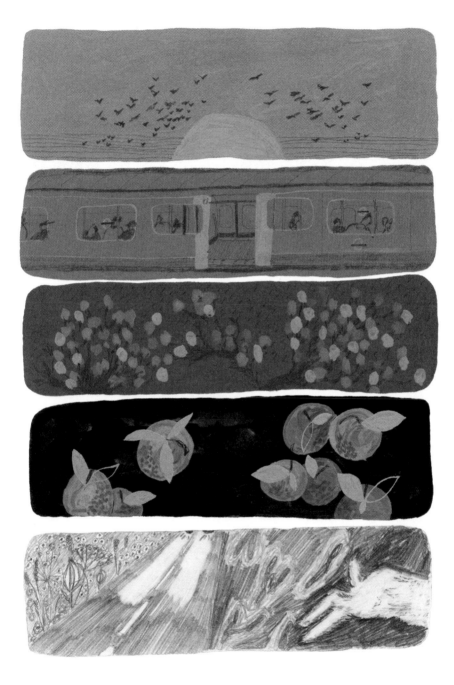

I WOULD LIKE TO EXPLAIN IT
AS THE THINGS THAT STICK
TO US LIKE SMALL BURRS, THAT
CALL US TOWARD ACTION AND
FAIRNESS. IT IS THE SCATTERING
OF SEEDS AND THE PLANTING
OF FUTURES.

I'D LIKE TO EXPLAIN BEAUTY,
BUT I THINK THAT WOULD BE
A BIT LIKE TRYING TO
EXPLAIN LOVE.

(HERE GOES NOTHING,
HERE GOES EVERYTHING.)

The following pages look at beauty in a variety of ways, thinking about how beauty has become the beauty of today, looking backward and looking forward. I would like for you to have questions more than I would like for you to have answers, but I will try to give you some of those too. I would like for you to get a bit lost, so perhaps check your watch, perhaps tie yourself to a piece of furniture with string so that you can find your way back easily. I would like for you to whisper some of your secrets in between the pages, and for the things you read to return to you often—on a Tuesday afternoon in July, perhaps.

ANCIENT
BEAUTY

I think a lot about what our earliest ancestors found beautiful.

Maybe it would have been something from the natural world, like a moonrise.

(Did somebody decide that the moon was beautiful and we all just went along with it? I don't mind if that's the case but nevertheless I'd like to know.)

Yes, maybe a moonrise, or a low tide, or a red sky at night. Did we always think those things were astonishing? Certainly we have paid more attention to the dances of the natural world in the times gone by than most of us do now.

We used to measure our bodies against seasons and harvests and rain, and now we measure our- selves against SCHEDULES and FITTED CABINETS.

If we first found beauty in natural things maybe that's why we still, despite all the noise, feel that we should pay good attention to them—why we are still delighted by snowfall and the patterns birds make in the skies at dusk.

But maybe our ancestors didn't find all that much beauty in the efforts of the natural world. Maybe they found beauty in relationships, or moments of quiet—or loud—love, or a small carved object handed from one person to another.

There is a photograph tucked away somewhere at my parents' house that, I think, depicts me lost in something beautiful. I am around six years old and I am kneeling on grass in the garden, gently stroking a black-and-white rabbit. We are looking after the rabbit for a family friend who has probably gone on holiday or something else that sounded exotic and frivolous back then, and prior to that moment I had never stroked a rabbit. In the photograph I look pleasantly lost, and the rabbit looks content with things as they are. I think that was probably one of my first *felt* experiences with beauty.

I think about the *first* moment a human being experienced beauty, hundreds of thousands of years ago, and I think about my own experiences with beauty, and then it's hard not to think about everything in between.

WHAT IS IN BETWEEN:

THE RISING AND FALLING OF CIVILIZATIONS

CENTURIES OF KITCHEN FLOORS BEING CLEANED

ALL THE OBJECTS THAT HAVE EVER BEEN LOST

THE APPEARING AND DISAPPEARING
OF ENTIRE ISLANDS

VOLCANOES PAYING NO NOTICE TO ANYBODY ELSE

THE LOVE BETWEEN PEOPLE THAT SOAKS INTO THE
GROUND — THOUSANDS OF YEARS OF LOVE

HOW UNKIND WE ARE TO EACH OTHER

WHEN PEOPLE DECIDED ON SOCKS

DID ALL OF US, FOREVER, ALWAYS
WANT MORE ?

I wonder, if we were presented with everything the first early humans found beautiful, would we actually be able to *recognize* it all as beautiful?

Perhaps we wouldn't have the language to appreciate it anymore, wouldn't quite be able to see what our ancestors found so remarkable.

Suppose that we did though. I wonder if being able to see the beauty in what our earliest ancestors saw as beautiful would change what we are doing and valuing and running toward.

Everyone always says how good and how right you are to be existing in the present, to live only in the now, but I think that to never look backward seems inadvisable. We're not very good at joining up long stretches of time, but maybe we should practice doing it more. Because if we could walk down a path that led us from the very first beauties to right now, to the minute that you're reading this sentence, perhaps many more things would become clear.

PERHAPS you WOULD CALL
THE WHOLE SURFACE aRea
OF YOUR BODY Beautiful
and BE aBLE to eMPatHIZe
WITH MORE SURFACe aReas
too — Be aBLe to accept
Beauty that Looks
DIFFERENT FROM YOUR
own IDeas
aBout IT,
the
accePt
not KnowIng and the
cHaos and tHe Fact tHat

tHeRe aRe Days WHen
you Just can't see tHe
Moon at aLL.

What do you believe to be some of your first experiences with beauty? Was there anything beautiful in yesterday? Have your definitions of beauty already changed over time? This timeline is for you to note down, or draw, where some of your earliest memories of beauty sit in time.

A handful of mine:

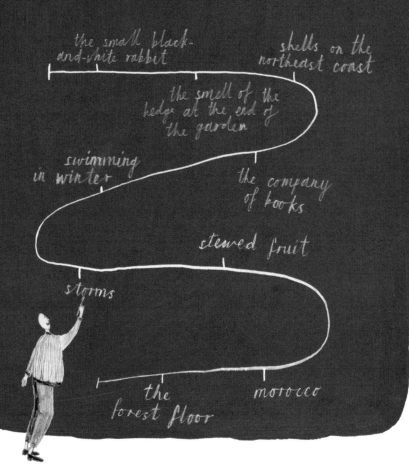

the small black-and-white rabbit

shells on the northeast coast

the smell of the hedge at the end of the garden

swimming in winter

the company of books

stewed fruit

storms

the forest floor

morocco

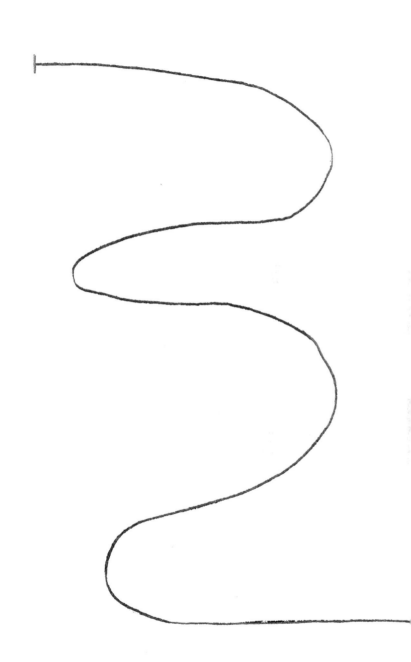

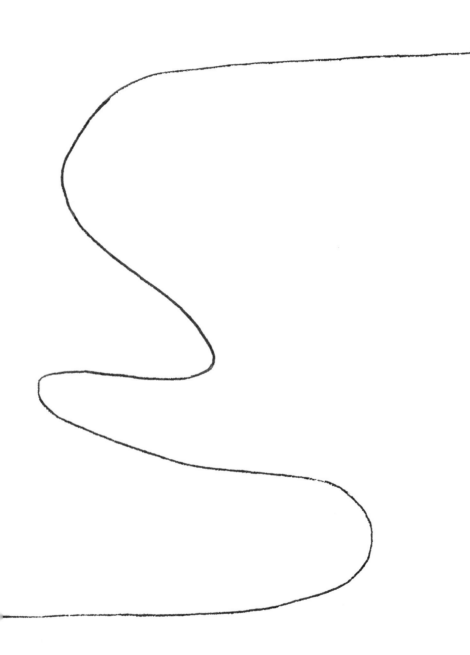

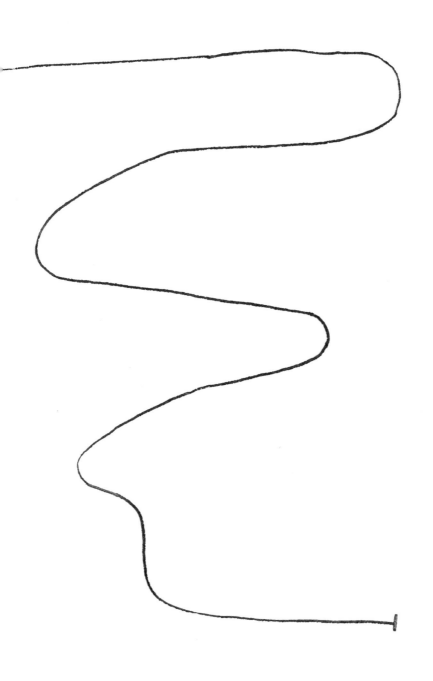

THE GOLDEN RATIO

As civilizations rose and fell, people began to have firm ideas about what beauty was and what it wasn't.

Mathematicians since ancient Greece have studied the properties of something called the golden ratio (also known in the 1500s as divine proportion).

What the golden ratio *looks* like depends on what it is being used for, but in art and architecture its application results in paintings that appear oddly pleasing and buildings that we are simply attracted to without knowing why.

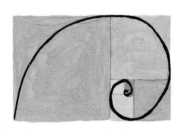

(Easiest — or a bit simpler — to understand using the golden ratio when it's viewed as the golden rectangle, or the golden spiral.)

The ratio can be applied to any geometric form—rectangles, circles, pyramids, prisms—and has been used in the work of countless architects and artists from Leonardo da Vinci to Salvador Dalí, who believed that these proportions would ensure the most aesthetically beautiful result. It can be seen in many of the paintings by Georges Seurat, in Michelangelo's ceiling in the Sistine Chapel, in da Vinci's famous work *The Last Supper*, in the Parthenon in Athens, and in the Egyptian pyramids.

Below are some examples of what this supposedly divine golden ratio looks like:

Man Leaning on a
Parapet

Georges Seurat
ca. 1881

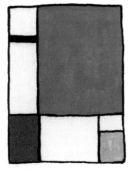

Composition with Red,
Blue and Yellow

Piet Mondrian, 1930

The Parthenon
Athens, Greece

The Great Wave off Kanagawa
Katsushika Hokusai
ca. 1829 - 1833

This mysterious ratio of proportion was—and still is—used to analyze the beautiful or not beautiful properties of everything, from the natural world to business models and computer programming.

In nature the golden ratio appears in situations like the leaves of plants; in their spiraling, ordered arrangements. The petals on flowers, the seeds of sunflowers, and pine cones.

(You need to look closely to see this.)

nautilus shell

sunflower

In 2010 the journal *Science* reported that the golden ratio is present at the atomic scale. I'm not sure exactly what that means, but I do know that we are all made of atoms, and if the supposedly most beautiful golden ratio is found in things that are atom-sized, then the answer to whether or not we can ourselves be inherently beautiful is surely yes.

The world is held together by tiny, beautiful things. Some are so invisible or silent that you may never see or understand them, but they are there.

SOME OTHER TINY, BEAUTIFUL THINGS:

A LADYBUG EATING APHIDS FROM A PLANT STEM AT 3 O'CLOCK IN THE AFTERNOON; BRAKING SUDDENLY FOR A BIRD; A NEIGHBOR KNOCKING TO ASK WHETHER YOU WANT HALF OF A LOP-SIDED CAKE; THE SPIDERWEBS THAT ARE QUICKLY BRUSHED AWAY; A SINGLE STONE SHIFTING ON A RIVERBED, A BLURRY PHOTOGRAPH TAKEN JUST BEFORE EVERYTHING CHANGES; THE DANCES WE DO TO AVOID HURTING THE FEELINGS OF ONE ANOTHER.

WHETHER YOU FIND IT IN PASSING
OR LOOK FOR IT SPECIFICALLY,
DRAW OR DESCRIBE SOMETHING
BEAUTIFUL THAT IS SMALLER
THAN A SMALL ORANGE.

ON THE FOLLOWING PAGE, DRAW
OR DESCRIBE SOMETHING
BEAUTIFUL THAT IS ABOUT
AS SMALL AS A PAPER CLIP.

(THE WORLD IS HELD
 TOGETHER BY tiny
BEAUTIFUL THINGS, AND
 IN tHE case OF PAPERCLIPS
THIS IS QUITE LITERAL.)

BEAUTY IN THE NATURAL WORLD

While people created art and built cities and argued about golden ratios, the natural world continued existing. In Western colonial cultures, a renewed appreciation for the beauty of the natural world grew steadily throughout the seventeenth and eighteenth centuries—I imagine this as wealthy white society looking out at rugged or serene landscapes and saying things like *hmm* and *aah* and *yonder*.

But WHY Does THeRe seem To Be a universal appeal wHen IT comes To ceRTain Types OF LanDscaPe, anD HOW DO We know THat sunseTs aRe BeautIFUL ?

For some, natural beauty means the absence of perfection or repetition, but for others it is the widespread, symmetrical repetition that is so pleasing, so meaningful, so memorable—both havoc and order are spread richly throughout the natural world.

OVER TEN YEARS AGO A PSYCHOLOGY PROFESSOR WORKING IN TOKYO, SHIGERU WATANABE, FOUND THAT JAVA SPARROWS COULD DISTINGUISH BETWEEN HARMONIOUS AND DISCORDANT MUSIC, PREFERRING THE MORE TUNEFUL TUNES, AND PERHAPS THAT IS ALL HUMAN APPRECIATION IS TOO.

DO WE ALWAYS PREFER THE HARMONIOUS TO THE DISCORDANT, WHATEVER THAT DISTINCTION MIGHT LOOK LIKE TO US?

IT IS NOT MY PLACE TO SAY THAT THE MUSIC YOU'RE LISTENING TO SOUNDS TERRIBLE. ON THAT NOTE, HARMONY IS VERY MUCH ITS OWN KIND OF BEAUTIFUL, AND IT LOOKS AND FEELS LIKE DIFFERENT THINGS TO ALL OF US. FOR ME, HARMONY IS FOUND IN THE WAY TREE BRANCHES WILL SOMETIMES GROW CURVING AROUND TO HOLD EACH OTHER, THE WAY RAIN DISAPPEARS INTO THE SURFACE OF THE SEA, THE SITTING AND SIGHING IN FRONT OF LANDSCAPES THAT ARE TOO LARGE TO COMPREHEND, AND WHEN WE HAVE ENOUGH ENERGY LEFT TO DANCE AT THE END OF THE DAY.

We must not forget, though, while oohing and aahing about the natural world, that none of it has evolved *for* us. That it is, in many ways, a marvelous coincidence that we would find any of it beautiful at all: flowers are not here purely for us to behold, trees do not grow because of us (more like in spite of at this point), and as far as I know, there are no measurable benefits to gazing at clouds. We, too, have evolved, have learned and been conditioned to appreciate many natural sceneries and forms, although I'm not sure that the same could be said the other way around—if you asked a tree, would it find you beautiful? If we could understand the discussions of sea creatures, would they have anything to say about the beauty of humans?

WITH ALL OF THIS IN
YOUR MIND, CHOOSE A

DAY TO WAKE BEFORE
THE DAWN.

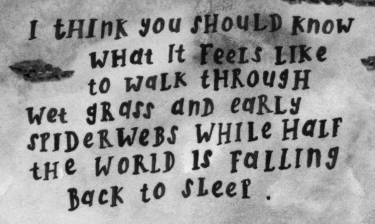

I THINK YOU SHOULD KNOW
WHAT IT FEELS LIKE
TO WALK THROUGH
WET GRASS AND EARLY
SPIDERWEBS WHILE HALF
THE WORLD IS FALLING
BACK TO SLEEP.

OR TO WALK THE STREETS WHILE THEY ARE MISSING THE HEAVY NOISE OF PEOPLE, TO NOTICE HOW THE TARMAC SMELLS BEFORE THE LIGHT TOUCHES IT, TO WATCH AS THE DAY BEGINS TO BE COLORED IN WITH THE DETAILS.

IF YOU'RE NOT WATCHFUL, THE WONDERFUL IS MADE MUNDANE. BUT ON A GOOD DAY THE MUNDANE CAN BE MADE MIRACULOUS.

To think that only three hundred years ago scholars were seriously discussing the possibility that storks spent their winters on the moon. and we now know that they do not spend their winters on the moon, and we also know that the rufous hummingbird, a bird weighing one tenth of an ounce, makes a four-thousand-mile migration, and that there are spiders drifting about the atmosphere attached to homemade silk balloons.

BEAUTY AS DEFINED BY ART MOVEMENTS AND ARTISTS

Sometimes I like to sit in galleries and museums and just notice how long people stand motionless in front of *art*.

ARE tHey tHInKIng anytHIng
WHILe tHey ftanD tHeRe?
aRe tHey Juft ftanDIng tHeRe
Because tHey tHInK tHat Is
WHat tHey SHOULD DO?
aRe tHey Juft ftanDIng tHeRe
Because I'M LOOKIng at tHeM?
aRe tHey HavIng an ePIPHany?

Most, if not all, artists are occupied with the depiction, meaning, or resolution of beauty. When you consider that the history of art might reach back, oh, well, perhaps a million and a half years, there is understandably a great deal of variation in the practicing artist's definition of beauty.

Beauty in art has been many
things: teardrop-shaped flint,
images drawn in dust and rock,
formal portraits illustrating wealth,
formal portraits illustrating scarcity,
pastel-colored landscapes, straight
lines, sculptures absent of
straight lines, and on and on.

Wave
Barbara Hepworth
plane wood with strings
1943-1944

Curved Form (Bryher II)
bronze
Barbara Hepworth, 1961

If anything, this fickle swaying history demonstrates how much beauty within art overlaps with the beauty in culture and with time, expectation, memory, and status. Status, yes, because we seem to find and accept without question a lot of beauty inside contexts that are overseen by the notion of prestige: museums, temples, galleries, the rooms of our own homes. Endless connections run like stinging ants between beauty and prestige, between beauty and attentions, affections.

Is everything that could be considered an art form a form of beauty? Static visual beauties (paintings and sculptures and such) leave a lot out, but beauty in art can be more fluid and unusual and short-lived — installations that wash away with the tides of the sea, exhibitions that are left to dissolve in the sunlight, thousands of people gathering to dance the same dance.

All acts of curation are also utterings about beauty, whether that is the curation of priceless paintings for stark white walls, or the curation of tiny yellow shells from a beach in northern

France for a windowsill, or someone taking a photograph of a single tree every morning for ten years.

The curation of beauty can look like so many things, and is often quite unexpected, requiring a certain amount of _looking_.
Feathers tucked into fenceposts by passing people, the objects on a coworker's desk, seeds organized neatly in a greenhouse, bookshelves, stacked-up stones on beaches, the arrangement of produce on market stalls.

As you move between your days, try to notice the curation of beauty — small curation, large curation, personal curation, and accidental curation.
You could take photographs of these curations, or note them down here with words, or with a sketch.

Perhaps you will be encouraged to curate beauty of your own, in your home or garden or on the route you walk to work each day. A shelf or a bed-side table can swiftly become a small museum, collecting objects that hold meaning and beauty for you and you alone. (On the following page I have included a few of my own museums from both past and present to give you a couple of starting points.)

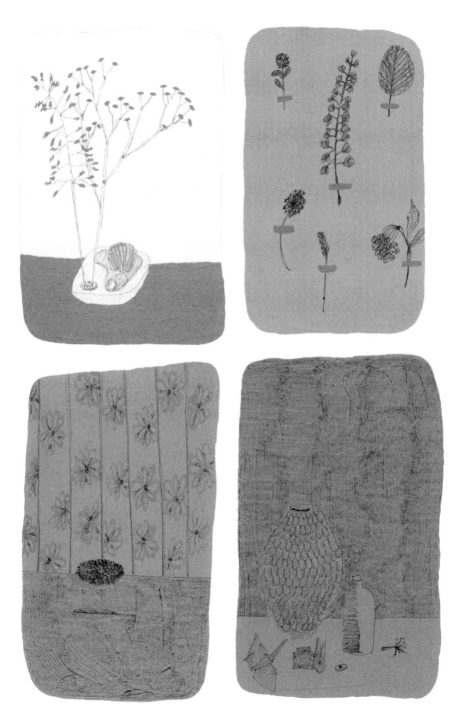

BEAUTY YOU CAN TRANSLATE AND BEAUTY YOU CANNOT

We go to great lengths to explain beauty, to prove it, but the thing is that the more you try to immortalize something, the more you might risk losing sight of it completely.

DO WE ONLY LOVE THINGS WHEN WE UNDERSTAND THEM?

ONLY LOVE THINGS WHEN WE MISUNDERSTAND?

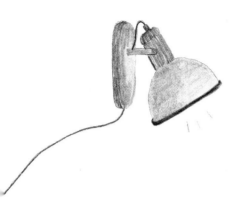

Sometimes we try to form words to encircle beauty. We try to translate our experiences of it into something others can understand and nod at. But it is not always possible to articulate beauty in a truly satisfactory way, because we each have our own relationship with the word *beauty*, because the texture of memory and meaning is never the same twice.

WHILE IT CAN BE DIFFICULT
TO WRAP LANGUAGE AROUND
BEAUTY, FOR IT TO HOLD ON TO
BEAUTY IN THE WAY OUR
HEARTS AND OUR NOSTALGIA
CAN, WORDS THEMSELVES
CAN BE A SOURCE OF SPECIFIC
AND GENUINE BEAUTY.

WORDS CAN LEAD US TO
NOTICING, LETTING US KNOW
THAT THERE IS SOMETHING
BEAUTIFUL THAT WE
MIGHT WANT TO LOOK
OUT FOR, AND ALSO
REMINDING US TO
GO MORE GENTLY.

If you begin to peel languages apart a little bit, all sorts of beautiful words fall out, with many of them being very precise, very poetic, very of place and time and landscape, of people.

There is, for example, an English dialect word, *smeuse*, that refers to a gap in the base of a hedge where a small mammal has been passing back and forth.

It often takes a word for us to realize that something might carry beauty, that we might wish to call it beautiful.

In Italian, it doesn't seem like a coincidence that the word for beauty, _bellezza_, rhymes with the word for slowness, _lentezza_.

Here is a space for words or phrases or murmurs that have meant something to you, that return to you without warning, that you like to carry around, that feel astonishing or simply notable:

Yesterday evening, while eating biscuits and watching a short film in which a man with a soft Scottish accent talks in an existential and mildly reassuring way over very close-up footage of insects, I received a call from my sister, who at this point I haven't seen in over a year although she only lives across a small piece of sea. On the call I learned that her fiancé had injured his elbow. The doctor they saw at twelve something at night provided a course of antibiotics and ibuprofen, and when asked about taking ibuprofen in the context of potentially contracting COVID-19, he replied with:

"That is far too much speculation."

Which is a phrase I liked immediately, and I am henceforth repeating it to myself when anxiety gets out of control, when I cannot work because I'm worrying myself flat, generally when I'm getting nowhere. I respond to myself with:

"That is far too much speculation."

Because it's completely true and because I can't squirm out of its firmness—we speculate so much, all the time, about everything, and it isn't often very helpful or calming or generous toward ourselves.

"THIS IS FAR TOO MUCH SPECULATION,"

I now say to myself each time I'm waiting to hang up a phone call, waiting until the total elapsed seconds are a multiple of eleven before pressing *end* to prevent anything bad from happening. "This is far too much speculation."

HISTORICALLY
CHANGING
BEAUTY

Until relatively recently, most of us had more pressing things to think about than our reflections in the mirror, but during the twentieth century that changed.

Following the First World War, the attitudes of the American public toward buying things were frugal ones, and purchases were made out of necessity—spending and shopping (consuming) were not yet viewed as *activities*. This changed during the 1920s with too much supply and too little demand, and over the next decades two Austrian-born men wielded serious influence within and upon the twentieth century—for largely unfortunate reasons.

One of these Austrian men* was interested in crowd psychology and preoccupied with creating the "perfect consumer." He discovered the predictable power of advertising products as symbols of identity and status, and as a consequence, the actual functions of products would become mostly irrelevant.

---

* Edward Bernays

The other Austrian man,* previously a psychoanalyst who lived down the road from Sigmund Freud in Vienna, was the author of disappointingly consumerist titles like *The Strategy of Desire*, in which he wrote things like "every new acquisition represents an enrichment of our personality." In other words, he was telling people that buying *things* made you more interesting. It was this man who created a direct link in the minds of the American public between consumption and pleasure, growing and cementing a widespread belief that consumption could be an activity or an occupation in its own right.

Marketing and advertising begin to look murky, and out of this murkiness a shiny new myth is created—that to be happy, to be successful, and to belong, people need to buy *things*. So hey! presto! the American consumer culture (and with it, beauty ideals) begins to spread like a sickly sweet jam to the rest of the planet.

Today, the world over, what is sold to every last one of us is a standardized, homogenized, westernized image of beauty. An unattainable one, of course, so that people never stop feeling dissatisfied or unhappy, so that they keep purchasing the empty promises contained within gelatinous eye creams, uncomfortable shoes, and louder car engines.

---

* Ernest Dichter

* MAY CAUSE FEELINGS OF NOT-

GOOD - ENOUGH

THIS DEFINITION OF BEAUTY IS UNFEELING, AND THE STANDARDS ARE CHANGED ALL THE TIME — KEPT IMPOSSIBLE SO THAT PEOPLE THE WORLD OVER AND FROM ALL THE CORNERS OF ALL THE SOCIETIES WILL CONTINUE TO FEEL THAT THEY ARE NOT ENOUGH. PRIOR TO THE TWENTIETH CENTURY, THERE WERE MORE VARIED AND INTRICATE DEFINITIONS OF WHAT MIGHT BE BEAUTIFUL, AND THESE COULD CHANGE AND SHIFT WITHOUT THE INTER-FERENCE OF ADVERTISING AND, INCREASINGLY, THE AMERICAN-EUROPEAN IDEAL. NOT MANY PEOPLE IN NOT MANY PLACES HAVE ESCAPED UNSCATHED.

This supposed one and only way of being beautiful has spread like wildfire — unstoppable, unpersuadable, and leaving behind confused people who are uncertain or sad when they catch sight of themselves in a mirror.

The devil of it is that if everybody woke up tomorrow and decided that they liked themselves exactly how they were, capitalism and everything clinging onto it would crumble like a piece of stale toast.

notice what happens
when you don't
look in the mirror
for a week (you
can cover mirrors
with paper or
flowers).

CONSIDER THE BEAUTY
IN THE WAY SOMEONE
MOVES THEIR HANDS, IN
HOW THEY LOOK OUT AT
HORIZONS, IN THE
ARRANGING OF KNEES,
IN THE   WAY
FEET   ARE
RESTED,   THE
     UN-   EVENNESS
OF   SHOULDERS.

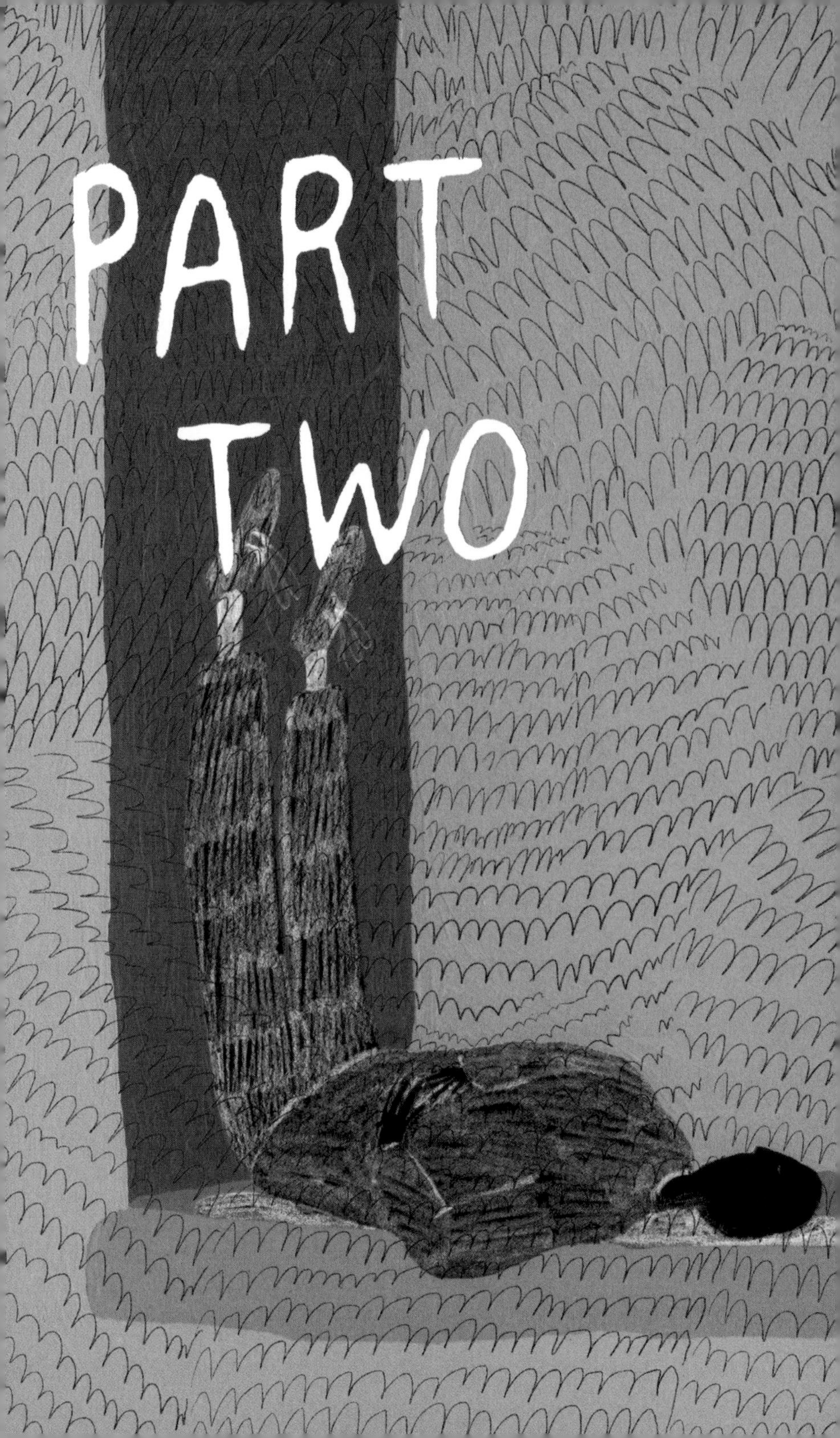
PART
TWO

UNREALISTIC
BEAUTY

Unrealistic beauty can
be insidious, heavy, or silencing.
It can be a stuck record,
sleepless nights, external
shouty things telling you
that you need to apologize for
the "things that", in fact,
make you radiant.

Unrealistic beauty is like a
predator that follows you around—
one that never gets tired
and will not let you sit down
to rest. It is like demanding
that trees blossom in the middle
of a glittering, naked-branch
winter.

Craving or obsessing over
unrealistic beauty is like
bailing water out of a
bottomless boat—the whole
vessel needs rebuilding.

We have been getting increasingly distracted by the unreal—by the conversations we no longer have in person, by our reflections, by the advertised promises of better, next, other, more.

When we desire the unreal, when we spend so much time running after it, so much time dissatisfied, we stop being able to notice the *real things*, the things that hold the universe together, that hold us to the universe. These things look like sugar crystals stuck to a saucer, birds landing on water, the difference between trees and telegraph poles, finding notes in secondhand books, the way a nettle leaf won't sting you if you pinch it tightly, the ridiculousness of layer cakes, breezes through thin curtains, the way a loved one looks at you when you're standing in dappled sunlight.

PLACE THIS BOOK DOWN — CLOSED,
OPEN FACE-UP, OPEN FACE-DOWN —
AND GO OUTSIDE. IT DOES
NOT MATTER WHAT THE
CLOCKFACE SAYS. IF YOU
CANNOT GO OUTSIDE, COME BACK
TO THIS PAGE LATER, OR OPEN
A WINDOW WIDE AND
POSITION YOURSELF AS
CLOSELY TO THE OUTSIDE
AS YOU CAN.

(If you are reading this
book outside, you are
currently a beauty being
noticed by   others.)

IS THERE A SUN?
IS THERE A MOON?
IF YOU FEEL YOU CAN, OPEN YOUR EYES.
IS THERE WARM SUNLIGHT ON YOUR SKIN
OR THE DAMPNESS OF RAIN SENT DOWN BY CLOUDS?
IS THERE A WIND
TRYING TO GO AROUND YOU?
PERHAPS YOU ARE IN A STORM,
PERHAPS YOU ARE IN THE MORNING SUN,
PERHAPS YOU WILL TAKE A FEW
MOMENTS TO FEEL THE WEATHER
ON MOST DAYS NOW.

WHY IT IS SO DIFFICULT FOR BEAUTY TO MEAN ANYTHING

And so it is difficult, now, for beauty to mean anything for many people.

It is difficult because there is no such thing as *better than* when it comes to beauty, because we learn and are conditioned to appreciate such limited ideas of beauty. It is difficult because you have been through a lot.

Difficult because beauty is quite like the sea, in that it makes up such a large percentage of the surface, in that it is not a problem to be solved, not a question to be answered, in that we forget sometimes that it is there, or that we cannot bear to look at it any longer. It has been said that beauty is not commonly found at the close of things, but rather at openings and edges and middles.

Exceptions to Beauty at the closing of things:

the fall of a theater curtain

windows pulled closed against strong rain

flowers curling up for the night

Beauty is difficult because unlike what we have been told, there is no neat solution, no last word, no shopping list, no instructional leaflets. Definitions of it cannot be cemented, computerized, or even constant. And so often it is in between things rather than the things themselves.

It is difficult because beauty can last for three seconds or three million years, because some things can be beautiful in the dark but not in the light, because some things can be beautiful now but not beautiful later.

It is difficult for beauty to mean anything because we are told a thousand times a day that for something to be beautiful it has to be beautiful not only to you but also to other people. Tradition and authority have designated some things as beautiful and some things as not beautiful, and for the most part we go along with this. We are encouraged to compare our beauties and bodies to those of others, to hold them up and point out all of the places that seem lacking.

The forgotten truth of the matter is that if you find something to be beautiful, this is *enough*. You do not need other people to confirm that beauty, to validate it; in fact, you do not necessarily need to utter a word about your beauties to anyone else at all.

The only way for beautiful to mean everything is when the edges are defined by *you*.

"I HAD RULED OUT PALM TREES AS OBJECTS OF BEAUTY AND THEN ONE DAY DISCOVERED I HAD MADE A MISTAKE."

— ELAINE SCARRY

BEAUTY SHOULD NOT HAVE CEILINGS

When you see yourself reflected, whose beauty do you see? Your own beauty or someone else's idea of it?

One single type of beauty should not speak on behalf of—or silence—other types of beauty, but that is exactly what has been happening. With a whole universe around us, isn't there more? With a whole universe around us, why are we listening to a century-old, made-up definition from two Austrian men?

To a large extent we are no longer free to choose which parts of the word *beauty* mean something to us, and we are the only creatures where that is so. Everything else in the world is free to choose its own beauty—honeybees choose their flowers without worrying what other honeybees will think or wondering whether visiting a particular lilac tree will increase their social standing—but for us it has become complicated, and without necessarily knowing that we are doing it, we often choose our beauties based on what other people might think or how they might judge us.

How strange to have seemingly
progressed through all of this
difficult and terrible history
and to not be very liberated
at all, not be free to choose
what is beautiful to us without
judgment from others.

Our choices begin to look less
like choices and more like
consumption, and our desires
start to resemble trapped
desires rather than independent
ones.

We get stuck wanting things,
wanting beauty, simply because
everything and everyone
else seems to be pointing
in a certain direction — we
are very often weighed down
by definitions of beauty we
did not ask for and that
do not benefit or serve us.

Of course, we now use the word *beautiful* quite casually to mean many other related things, like "good" or "excellent," or to try and persuade someone that yes, they really do look fine in that new sweater. Our use of *beautiful*, it has been argued by some, has become frivolous, although I would argue that it has not, and that frivolity itself can be quite a beautiful thing. Yes, beautiful is saturated, very saturated, but it is our definitions that need to change, not how often we use the word.

Our individual languages often lack adequate words for the variety of beauties we are faced with, and so naturally one begins to wonder, if we used the word *beautiful* from morning until night, what would it mean? And if the definition were to be left completely open like the crater of a volcano, would it be empty of meaning or full?

BEAUTY DOES NOT HAVE A CEILING.

At the moment we are looking again and again in the same small corner for beauty. We pick up the same stones over and over, looking at their undersides and wondering why nothing has changed, why we feel the same.

If you can see beyond this small corner, beyond the ordinary and culturally stuck definitions, something else starts to come into view, and that thing is an array of delicate spectacular that you won't be able to articulate—at first.

This, this thing you are struggling to speak of, is the new beauty. A beauty that asks you to slow down to your animal speeds and to notice when the stars are looking sad.

SOME BEAUTIFUL THINGS I NOTICED WHEN I SLOWED DOWN

The place in a small town where I sometimes buy groceries is usually full of people in good moods—possibly because they consume organic things, I'm not sure. One morning I walked in and there was an air of *jubilance* about the place because someone had lost their wedding ring while drying their washed hands on paper towels and an employee had later found it while emptying the wastebasket. This news had transformed the feeling of the day for everyone there, filled it with potential and human goodness and a sense that things will work out all right in the end.

I listened to council workers emptying the monstrous community glass recycling bin up the road, which was not deafening in the way it would be if one were standing too close, but instead from a distance sounded like a gentle, glittering rain.

As I walk up the library steps, I see one of the librarians outside wielding a fifteen-foot-ish, thin wooden pole, looking as if he is perhaps intending to direct a gondola, and I make a comment along the lines of "that looks interesting" as I approach. He thinks that I'm referring to the large new poster of the actor Belinda Lang that has appeared on the outside wall, but I make it clear that I'm referring to whatever he is doing with the wooden pole. He informs me that he is trying to clear the fronts of the security cameras because over time spiderwebs and flies in spiderwebs and all manner of things begin to obscure the image. He seems content, and I wonder whether I will ever see anyone attempting to clean security cameras in quite the same way again.

THERE ARE TWO MIGHT-
AS-WELL-BE-EMPTY CANS
OF PAINT UNDER THE STAIRS—
THE COLORS ARE CALLED
NATTERJACK AND *KITTIWAKE*
— AND IF THE TEMPERATURE
IN THE HOUSE CHANGES
                    TOO MUCH,
                    I CAN HEAR
                    THE SOFT

"PLUNK"
(PING? PLINK?)
OF THE METAL LID OR THE
METAL SIDES SHIFTING TO MAKE
THEMSELVES MORE COMFORTABLE
AS THEY GET TOO HOT, AS THEY
GET TOO COLD.

Huge banks of oxeye daisies
line the roadsides, freckled
carpets of yellow and white
that seem to last
longer than my own
certainty about
anything.

As vehicles drive past them,
the long flower stems get pulled
one way and then the other, in
unison. Driving behind a large
bus the other day, I
watched how the flowers all
danced madly as the bus sped
by – in delight, in panic, in
boredom, I could
not tell.

This morning I ate strawberries in the bathtub, which felt in equal measure unnecessary and essential and luxurious and absurd, and into the bath I'd put some kind of citrusy thing containing orange oil and who knows what. Now, as I walk through a forest on a small circular loop, it occurs to me that this orange oil might be the reason why it seems like all of the insects are following me—that, or it's finally summer.

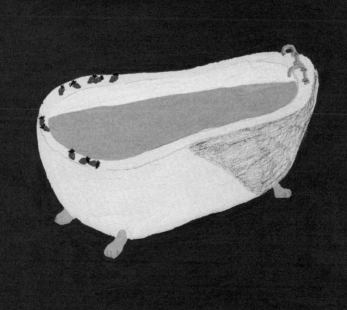

For one day, do everything just a little bit more slowly than you normally would and notice what happens to beauty.

Notice what collects at the corners of things.

If you can, find a bee and watch as it decides on flowers, decides on directions, decides whether you are a safe place

to land.

FICTIONAL
BEAUTY

(I'm writing this sitting in a wooden chair next to a pond, and a few moments ago a minute reddish-brown spider appeared at the top of the page. I encouraged it gently from the paper to my finger to the arm of the wooden chair and then moved my left elbow so that the tiny spider could continue deciding on its direction unimpeded. It may be on my sweater by now—I don't know.)

Fiction and beauty too often share the same definition. The definition of fiction is "something invented by the imagination or feigned," and if you think about the perceptions of and the discussions about beauty in the last ninety years—and probably the last nine thousand years—there are some alarming parallels.

Fictional things are made up. They are pulled out of thin air, and the same could be said for our present-moment definition of beauty. Such a beauty, what it *is* and is *seen to be*, is decided on by a small number of people with money. It isn't a very imaginative thing to demand others see things in the way that only you want.

The fact that fiction and beauty often get labeled as the same thing is a problem I'm not willing to leave alone. For example, when we read a fictional book, we do not expect it to be factual. So why are we still drinking up fictional beauty as fact? There are really just two words to answer the question: money and power

(contrary to what some people say, money and power are never in and of themselves beautiful).

The people who declare the rules of modern beauty are scared that you and I will wake up tomorrow and realize that we've been reading someone else's book on the subject.

we can,
in fact,
write
our own
books
about
Beauty.

There is nothing wrong with sharing an exclusive and limited view on beauty, but it is not fine to tell other people that their thoughts are invalid or unworthy. When we say, "That's not beautiful," what we mean, usually, is that someone or something is outside our own tiny boundaries of perceived beauty or rightness or acceptability. Who are we to tell someone that their own personal ideas of beauty are wrong?

This fictional beauty, the beauty we are sold, is exactly that—sold. Fictional beauty has a monetary value, and so we are left exposed and believing that we can acquire this beauty, save up for it, make it an ever-present, unchanging state of being that will live forever. But the new beauty, the types of beauty I am trying to explain and uncurl, do not have a value. These beauties cannot be bought or sold, and they definitely can't be found as companies on the stock market.

PERHAPS a question to ask
ourselves these days,
surrounded on all sides
by advertising and
dissatisfaction, is:

"Does this supposedly beautiful
thing have a price?"

          OR

" am I being asked to buy beauty?"

It is not our desires for beauty
that are the problem — the
problem is that our desires
have been hung out to dry
in a scorching sun by a
commercial culture that
declares nobody is good
enough just as they are.

Desires can be beautiful in themselves, but perhaps the objects or the products or the procedures or the backdrops that produce such desires are not beautiful.

I think we must learn to question where our desires for beauty are coming from, and whether we are paying dearly for them. It isn't that different from how more of us now routinely ask where our food comes from, or where our facts come from – we need to start talking about where our ideas of beauty are coming from, because right now a lot of us are troubled, a lot of us are thinking that our unique and diverse types of faces, bodies, or lines are not fit for purpose.

We are reading
modern beauty as fact,
when it is most absolutely
fiction. And once you
realize, once you
understand that you
don't have to read
those books anymore, the
world looks remarkably
different — in many ways,
it looks more remarkable.

(It is plenty
for now to simply watch
a bee landing clumsily
on flower after flower,
without having to explain
away everything that is
delicate and important.)

WRITE OR DRAW
OR FIND SOME-
THING BEAUTIFUL
AND THEN MAIL IT
TO SOMEONE IN
AN ENVELOPE

with no
accompanying
explanation—
see what it
feels like
to give
beauty away.

WHERE THE BEAUTIFUL THINGS GO

How can we be surrounded by beauty and yet struggle to feel it? How does a person go in search of a new definition of beauty when the modern internet world seems intent on drowning out any attempts at different? And if you want to write your own book of beauty, how do you begin?

Beauty leaves us because at some point we stop looking for it, because we stop paying attention to the right and good kind of beauty. It leaves because we become so focused on large futures that we forget about the small and lovely worlds standing in front of us. Beauty leaves because we are led to believe that we can fill up our human hearts with *stuff*, that relief and meaning will follow on from consumption and careers—I don't think I need to tell you, but it doesn't work like that.

Our habits, words, and behaviors lead us down various paths, and we can be so focused on progressing down those paths with our heads high, or with our heads low, that we don't notice what we are passing on the way.

There are lots of things that can potentially inhibit or delay our finding and recognizing beauty—stress, overwhelm, despair, illness, loss, fear. The work—the true and difficult work—is seeking the beauty despite or even because of hard things. (I will talk more about this.)

Beauty leaves us because we are resting our heads on the wrong shoulders. It leaves because we are always rushing to cover up discomfort and pain, because we try to fill in all the gaps—in walls, in feelings, in other people, in endings. It leaves, but luckily for you and me it doesn't necessarily go very far, and so we stand an astonishingly good chance of finding it again.

"LET ME KEEP MY MIND ON WHAT MATTERS, WHICH IS MY WORK,

WHICH IS MOSTLY STANDING STILL AND LEARNING TO BE ASTONISHED."

— MARY OLIVER

FIND a BENCH —
SOMEWHERE,
anyWHERE — and SIt
on It, tHen WaIt
foR tHIngs to
HaPPen.
you can aLso waIt
foR notHIng to
HaPPen, But tHIngs
usuaLLy DO.

(the Most Recent tIMe
I DID tHIS, tHe tHIng
tHat Happened Was Me
gettIng BItten on My
Left ankLe By a
Mosquito.)

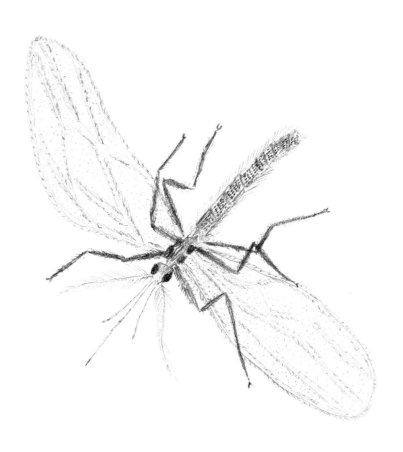

BEAUTY'S BIG REVEAL

THE INGREDIENTS OF BEAUTY

Knowing some of the ingredients of beauty can be an easier thing than attempting to recognize it as a whole. Once you know some of the ingredients—your own ingredients, not someone else's, although it can be good and necessary to appreciate other perspectives from time to time—beauty becomes more easily recognized, more prevalent, and more everywhere. One particular ingredient can lead you to something else, which can suggest another thing, and before you know it you're in conversation with everything beautiful.

For me some of the ingredients for beauty are light, slowness, and the kind of air temperatures that feel like honey. Others are solitude, circles, and close attention.

Very often it will be only one or two ingredients that cause us to notice beauty, but there are times when handfuls of them combine to make something overwhelmingly beautiful—we might call this the sublime, the awestruck, need-to-sit-down-to-breathe reverence. We don't get too many of these sublime moments, so it is very worthwhile being able to recognize them when they do come around.

The next time something seems beautiful to you, ask yourself why and see what comes to mind. Nothing may happen, and that is all right, too, but it is likely you will know—with varying degrees of clarity—which ingredients form that beauty. It might be a feeling or an aesthetic, or it might be something that reminds you of something else. It might be formed of the past, the present, or even the future. It might be details or a large sweep. When I asked a few people what their own ingredients of beauty were, or might be, I was provided with the following:

time, eggshells, soil,
citrus fruit, clean
teeth, prime
numbers, softness,
home, déjà vu,
vigilance, seabirds,
tingles, whispers,
hiding things from
oneself, dovetail
joints, **rest**,
overcast, tomorrow,
islands, bright sides,
liveliness, Kyoto,
just a little,
expeditions, arches,
you.

The point I'm trying to make is that beauty can be made up of, can come from, *anything*. Yes, it can help to identify some ingredients or components that make up your beauties, but even more than that you need only to be listening for it and to have interest in cultivating and caring for those things.

These two pages are
for you to note down
your own ingredients
for beauty, as organized
or as overlapping as you
like. Things like sensations,
times of day, objects, or
types of light:

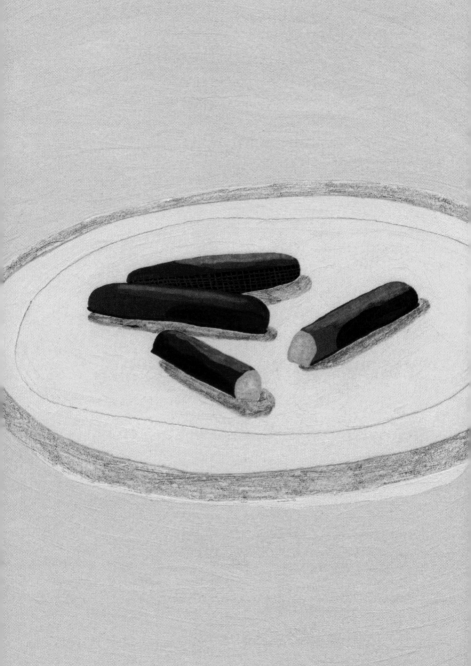

HOLDING ON TO BEAUTY WHEN LIFE UNRAVELS

We must now talk about holding on to beauty even when it's hard.

(To prepare myself for talking about this, I eat five chocolate biscuit fingers.)

I'm not sure whether the kind of beauty that exists in the midst of tragedy needs much in the way of an introduction, because you'll know about it, but it is certainly deserving of discussion and a looking into—the way you might peer into a small, curled flower, wishing to see further but not wanting to damage it in any way.

(That reminds me, I must go outside and visit the single yellow flower on my hip-height magnolia tree, which smells like citrus and answers.)

One of the hardest things we can choose to practice is finding beauty within the more difficult and unraveling parts of life.

It is not always possible, and there should be no pressure (we shouldn't feel that we *must* find beauty in these things), but the relationship between beautiful and awful can be astonishing, and with some noticing and some tenderness, we can grow in expansive and thoughtful ways as we live through the awful.

I'm talking about the beauty that never leaves, even within the confines of grief or illness or hardships too hard to name.

When we are consumed—partially or wholly—by the dark, it may be that we need to squint or use a magnifying lens to see the small pins of light, but they are there.

Finding beauty within the darker, damaging things does not alter the weight of them, but it can, if only for a second, provide reflection, provide breath, provide safe pockets in which to shed tears or fury or terror, glimmers to hang our hopes on like coat hooks in a hallway.

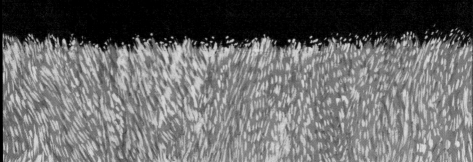

There is no ignoring that parts of life are awful, and everyone's awfuls will come in different shapes and intensities. We don't need to compare the awful, but we do need to talk about it more, especially about the awfuls that are not inherent and that need to be solved, fought against, abolished.

I am not here to compare the awful but to tell you that even the smallest beauties within conflict or catastrophe or the unimaginably cruel can be stitched together to form something of value.

The other day I saw a short video clip from Gaza, where people are fighting, firing missiles, and sending buildings into the ground. In this video two young children—perhaps five or six or seven years old—are holding up a glass jar containing an unremarkable pickle-sized fish that they have saved, and they talk excitedly about the fish while an unthinkable chaos surrounds their small hearts.

If we stitch together these tender human moments, we can then see the bigger, clearer, more truthful story, and perhaps come to know how a terrible or difficult situation is to be climbed out of, or learned from. Moments like this break us open but we must let them, because our human-ness floods out — ready to help, to heal, to tell kinder stories.

Because small green plants are able to grow up through snow, and the caretaker of the building wishes someone a happy Friday as they enter the elevator, and for the briefest of moments, all of humanity can be made gentle.

We don't need to run from these moments but rather keep watch over them as you might watch over a small, soft, rescued creature.

" HOWEVER IT IS ENCOUNTERED,

BEAUTY IS ALWAYS

AN EXCEPTION,

ALWAYS IN DESPITE OF.

THIS IS WHY

IT MOVES US. "

— JOHN BERGER

Find something to press
in between these pages,
like a leaf, or a grass
stem, or a fallen flower.

Close the pages shut
and put that beauty into
the dark, perhaps even
placing the book under
more dark, under heavy
things.

You might now leave
for a day or a few days,
or you might forget
about this book for
two weeks.

When you return, notice
what has happened to the
beauty, how the other side
of darkness is beautiful
in a different way from before.

<u>Unusual ways of</u>
<u>noticing time passing:</u>

GHastLY BRIGHt fLOWERS
Orening in tHe garDen

tHe SPReaD of SPIDeRWeBS

tHe COLLecTing of DusT on
tHe FLOOR anD THe surfaces

gRasses BecomIng
aLTeRnateLy MoRe
anD Less gReen

It RaIns foR
Days anD tHen
Doesn't

"Sometimes I see something so moving I know I'm not supposed to linger. See it and leave. If you stay too long, you wear out the wordless shock. Love it and trust it and leave."

— Don DeLillo

EVERYTHING I COULD FIND THAT WAS BEAUTIFUL

There are days when I feel a great sense of worrisome urgency and a sort of conviction that I must document all of the beautiful things. I feel panic because I know that I can never explain well enough why these things are important, and this is some of the reason why holding on to them for longer—as words, as paintings, as an image—seems so necessary. I am, though, getting better at remembering that I can hold on only briefly, then let go. I don't need to have evidence of the beautiful forever.

And yet there is also beauty in remembering, different from the beauty found in forgetting, and because I forget so much, there is something to be said—some of the time—for preserving. I want to be able to look back on beauties and notice how the texture of my self has changed over time, and be able to show those people I care about in a few years' time *oh, yes, look, this is when the trees blossomed.*

We want to keep hold of and pin down beauty in the way that we put effort into loving, into being loved—we wish for our lives to be witnessed. And in a funny way, beauty witnesses us just as much as we see it, perhaps more so. We want to keep hold because beauty is so often a porch light in the darkness.

HOW BIRDS CHOOSE TO SIT

AT THE APEX OF BUILDINGS

THE WAY SOME PEOPLE ALWAYS LEAVE

THEIR CLOTHES-PEGS ON THE LINE

WHILE OTHERS BRING THE PEGS

IN AND OUT EVERY TIME

the small,
faintly spotted
feathers
that
young
birds
lose

someone
cutting up
an apple
for
you

You taking off the hairs
that forever attach
themselves to my sweaters

Questions when it's raining

A physio once said my
spine moved immaculately

Someone consuming cereal
while on the phone

How sometimes there is
a single tree hugging the
horizon, or the ridge of
a hill

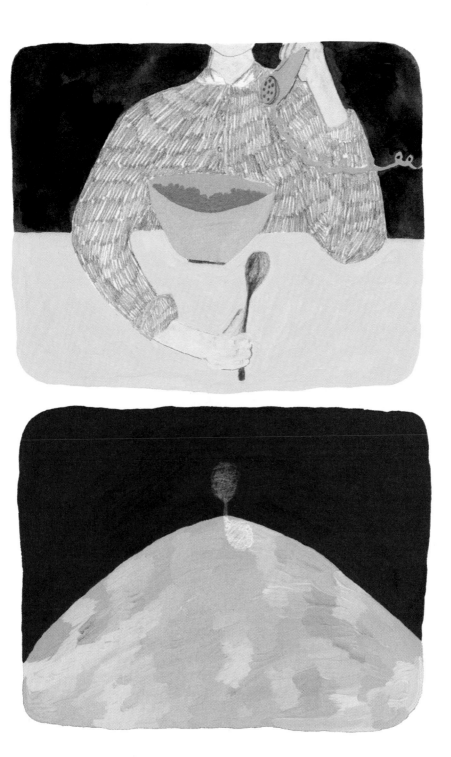

April sometimes
decides to keep you
cold

All roads lead to
other roads

The living green of
lake waters

The way you can rely on
a piece of fruit to mold

Floorboards warmed by
the sun

the determination of
flower bulbs while they
overwinter in cold
soil and

the way in which spring
can happen overnight

once when I was writing an
email autocorrect
changed the word
thoughts to ghosts
and I still think
about that sometimes

queues of traffic waiting
to turn left or right,
their indicators all
out of time, making
a terrible dance

Landscapes that look
like paintings

The way bright lights
remain behind your eyes
for a few moments after
closing them

The fingerprints and
lip marks left to linger
on drinking glasses

When it gets windy
enough that
seabirds drift
LIKE BITS OF PAPER
in the air

CLOUDS AT NIGHT,

THE ONES THAT LOOK LIKE OIL SPILLS

THE ELEGANCE OF

DANDELIONS

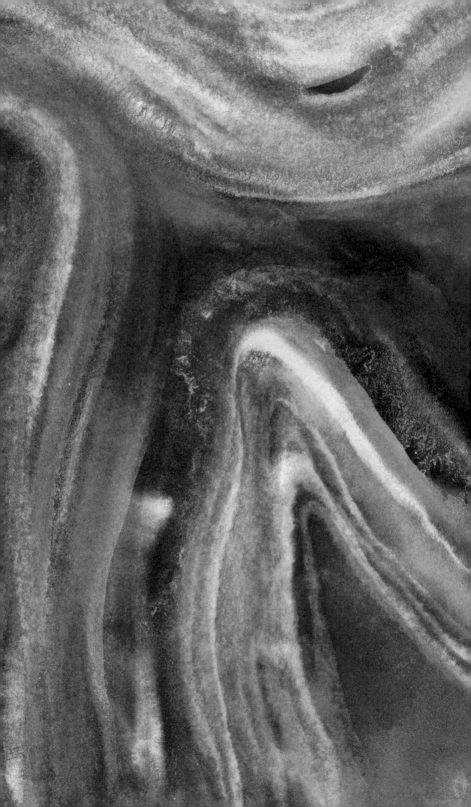

THE NEW
BEAUTY

Perhaps you decided at some point during these pages that you are ready for a new beauty.

Are you ready to shake off the definitions of beauty that are diminishing and undeserving of your light-filled body?

Where, now, to begin?

Does this feel like a beginning?

Does it feel like an end?

the new beauty, quite simply, does not make you feel terrible. it does not make you wonder whether you are enough. instead the new beauty serves as small miracles

of confirmation and clarity that you <u>are</u> enough, that you always were.

It does not have to be explained away to others, and it cannot be sold. The new beauty moves more slowly than the things you knew as beauty before. The new beauty is questioning the way things have been, the way things are, and putting forward ideas for futures in which we have more time to gaze at each other, more time to build cities with small stones beside the sea.

The new beauty is radical because it allows us to love ourselves in spite of being told not to; it is caring for yourself in whatever way that looks like for you—it is letting others love themselves without interruption or judgment or shame.

The new Beauty
is a fierce
noticing.

Much of the time
you can let it Be
wordless But on
occasional nights
it will Be shouting

curses at
the planets
you cannot
see.

THe new Beauty
eMBRaces symmetry
as a form of
equality,

SYMMetry as
a pull toward
fairness and
justness and
Protective of the fragile.

And spending time cultivating a new beauty does not mean that we wish to become more literally beautiful ourselves, but it will certainly cover our insides with everything beautiful. Our emotional interiors become more richly varied and understanding, and as individuals we stop needing to be so loud and central to everything. The new beauty moves us away from the overwhelmingly self-centered and toward a version of events where other important things—beauties, carefulness—can be placed at the center of our rotating.

The new beauty is a bit like catching glimpses of your own heart from the other side of a river. Inclusive beauty, nuanced beauty, beauty that only wants the best for you.

Perhaps you will find yourself at not be surprised to book, but I the end of the

would like for you to feel that you are, yourself, a beginning.

Begin at slow.

Begin at winter sunlight and the condensation that sweeps up from the edges of window frames.

Begin noticing beauty before breakfast, when you're hungry; begin with rest and warmth and trying to put worrying to one side so that even if just for half a day you can fill the other side with your goodness and your possibility and with sewing buttons back on.

Begin at noticing why your neck aches on the left, and then try not to feel frustrated when a sock goes missing in the machine.

Begin with watching a candle flame in the dark for five whole minutes, with letting yourself collapse when it gets too much—it is all too much these days, and often.

Begin with failing and with that being all right.

BEGIN WITH FORGIVING YOURSELF

BEFORE

YOU'VE EVEN   STARTED.

A BEAUTIFUL ENDING

There was never a particularly neat or simple way to end this, because as I said earlier in these pages, beauty is almost always an opening and not often a closing. To this effect, I would like the book to start all over again, before it's over, but with you writing it this time.

The following pages are for you to write, record, and witness a year of beauty, using the days and months as a structure but without any other limitations in terms of what gets included, or when, or how.

You can show the pages to nobody, or you can show the pages to many people, or you can show the pages only to your cat—the point, the main point at least, is that these pages are for *you*, to rewrite and redefine beauty in the way that you wish and need to.

The world is ready for its close-up, for its far-away, for you to notice it all.

Month of _____

M	T	W	T

Year _____

F	S	S

Notes:

Month of _____

M	T	W	T

Year ——

F	S	S

Notes :

Month of _____

M	T	W	T

Year ____

F	S	S

Notes:

Month of _____

M	T	W	T

Year ____

F	S	S

Notes:

Month of _____

M	T	W	T

Year ____

F	S	S

Notes :

Month of _____

M	T	W	T

Year _____

F	S	S

Notes:

Month of _____

M	T	W	T

Year ___

F	S	S

Notes:

Month of _____

M	T	W	T

Year _____

F	S	S

Notes:

Month of _____

M	T	W	T

Year ____

F	S	S

Notes:

Month of _____

M	T	W	T

Year ___

F	S	S

Notes:

Month of ____

M	T	W	T

Year ____

F	S	S

Notes:

Month of _____

M	T	W	T

Year _____

F	S	S

Notes:

Last night I drove for an hour to reach the end of the world, and everything there was beautiful. The end of the world was a beach made entirely from pieces of shell, countless billions of them, and in order to see the view from the end of the world, I had to wade through a small rivery bit and up a steep dune of shells. The view from the end of the world was shimmering and watery, and although good to be alone, it would have been better to share the ending with you.